LITTLE BI
OF POPADUBOP

THE JOURNEY OF LOVE

REV. DR. OSCAR P. GRANT

outskirts
press

Outskirts Press, Inc.
http://www.outskirtspress.com

ISBN: 978-1-9772-3775-0

Outskirts Press and the "OP" logo are trademarks belonging to Outskirts Press, Inc.

PRINTED IN THE UNITED STATES OF AMERICA

CAST

ALICE HARRIS

BROWN SUGAR HARRIS

LANGLY (LIEING)

EATING ETHEL

EVILIDA/OLD WOMAN

NAGATHA

HAGATHA

RAGATHA

MRS.FARNSWELL (ETHEL'S MOTHER)

CREEPLIE (EVILIDA'S SON)

DOGOODIE GOODIE THE GOOD WITCH OF MANEGO

WALKING DOG

KING MANEGO

QUEEN MANEGO

SOUL PATROL CAPTAIN

SOUL PATROL DANCERS

PRINCE MANEGO

MONSTER

SIMON THE STORYTELLER

FOREWORD

Wow! It's been thirty-one years since "Little Black Alice of Popadubop" premiered in Chicago with the Chicago Youth Repertory (you can read more about this theatre company by logging on to LittleBlackAlice.com). Little Black Alice toured from 1979-1982 in the Chicagoland area. We toured daycares, libraries, jails, hospitals, elementary, middle schools, and corporate invitations with over 250 documented performances and three casts of youth over five years.

I'm often asked how Little Black Alice was conceived and it came from a story my mother told me about a girlfriend she had in Grenada, Mississippi. We were both looking at a story on TV regarding information from "*The Civil Rights Documentation Project: the Grenada Movement, 1999 and 2000.*" My mother was relating the challenge with racism and the problems she faced in the summers she spent there with the family.

She had a close friend named Rudean who was a real talented dancer. Rudean was rather tall and awkward for her age. Also, she was teased because her hair was not straight and as my mother stated, the adults and many kids her age would say and tease her saying that she had nappy n***** hair and many other hurtful things. Rudean was a very lonely girl and often told my mother she was her only friend. That's the essence of the story of Little Black Alice. Only, I wrote hope for Little Alice, where my mother's friend left the planet under other terms.

I'd like to thank my mom and dad and my sister Paula for the support they gave me while in college and even now in spirit in getting this story told and produced. Ben White and Joan McCarty, the creators of the Youth Repertory Theatre Company with funding from the Department of Cultural Affairs and the Archdiocese of Chicago for giving me the opportunity to work with those at-risk youth. Robert Andrew Jenkins (choreographer) and Sabrina Diane Smith (director) are and will be two creative artists that I rely on. They put many final touches to the many drafts and performances that saying thank you is not enough. I can't forget my New York business partner and bud - Bruce C. Edwards for co-producing the New York production. Thanks, Bruce.

Thank you Rev. Dr. Kenner, Youth Rep Theatre, the Off-Broadway cast, the recent cast in Chicago, and the regional shows that I have given an opportunity to perform this wonderful vehicle for youth that feel unloved, lonely, and challenged by a world that does not understand them.

I have so many individuals more to thank but I've done more acknowledgements on the LittleBlackAlice.com website.

PRELUDE

IN THE FAR FUTURE, ACCORDING TO INTERGALTIC TIME, A PROPHECY WAS MADE THAT THE EVIL WITCH EVILIDA WOULD BECOME THE FIRST MALEVOLENT QUEEN OF THE GALAXY. THIS PROPHECY WOULD BECOME TRUE ... IF THE ONE CALLED LITTLE BLACK ALICE FREELY CAME TO MANEGO. FOR IT WAS KNOWN THROUGHOUT THE UNIVERSAL GALAXIES THAT LITTLE BLACK ALICE WOULD MAKE EVILIDA'S SOUL PATROL DANCERS UNBEATABLE IN ANY SOLAR SYSTEM. SO IT IS WRITTEN, SO LET IT BE PROCLAIMED FOR ALL THE GALAXIES TO BOW TO THE NEW MALEVOLENT QUEEN EVIL EVILIDA.

Chapter 1 – Your Word Has Power

SIMON, THE STORYTELLER, 12, happily sits on a color-changing fast-moving cloud, enjoying the beauty of the spinning universe. Simon is happy, funny, and a joy to be around.

SIMON

HELLO, BOYS AND GIRLS! I'm Simon, the Story Master, and I live in Storyville where Story Masters read the books you learn from in school to me. Story Masters are teachers who have wisdom. We all need wisdom to guide us to do the right thing. This story is called LITTLE BLACK ALICE.

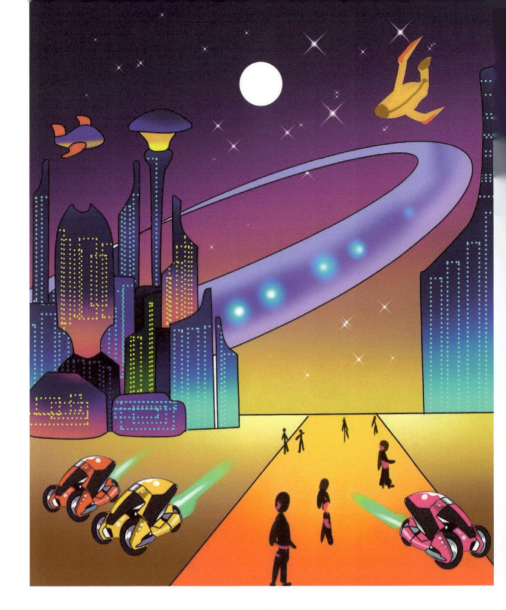

SIMON

The story of *Little Black Alice* takes place in two different towns in a faraway galaxy. The first town is called Popadubop (Papa-do-bop). Little Alice lives in the town of Popadubop. And Evilida, the wicked witch, lives in the magical, futuristic town of Manego (Man-egg-O). Manego has a good witch, a bad witch, a girl who has been hexed to snack a lot, a boy who has been hexed so he can't tell the truth, and a dog hexed to talk and walk like a human. Oh, and a strange monster that changes colors a lot.

Once upon a time, in the extremely near and far future according to the intergalactic time you are reading, there was a wonderful, hard-working family named Harris. The elderly Harris's were grandparents to their two granddaughters, Little Black Alice and Brown Sugar, who lived with them on their vegetable farm.

Their youngest granddaughter, Little Black Alice, loved to dance more than anything else in the world. When Little Alice danced, she felt all her problems disappear. Little Black Alice often felt very lonely. She missed her mother and father who both went back to the great Creator. Little Alice was often teased and bullied because her hair wasn't straight enough, and in the sun, her skin color would often change from brown to black. They called her hair nappy.

When Little Alice danced in competitions, she rarely lost the top prize. Recently, she won the INTERGALTIC GRAND NATIONALS Dance Competition. However, neither her grandparents nor her sister made it to the theatre to see her win the Grand Nationals. This happened once before to Little Alice. She remembered how the other girls teased her that no one loved her, not even her family. That made Little Alice so sad.

And now, again, she won the competition and was laughed at when the other dancers realized no one was there to cheer her on or see her win the trophy. When the bullies realized no one was there to support her, they tried to snatch the trophy from her and break it. Little Alice was so hurt. She just wanted someone to like her. She felt so alone. Little Alice was willing to give up dancing if it meant she would have a friend.

Every day, for weeks, Little Black Alice would go in her bedroom and look into her magic mirror, making the same wishes over the cosmic airwaves, "I wish, I wish, I were a lighter color. I wish, I wish, I had a friend. I wish, I wish my mama and daddy were not gone away. I wish... I wish... I wasn't so alone." Then Little Black Alice would just sit on her bed and cry. Little Alice didn't realize that she had to have support from her grandparents to help her deal with the bullies. She never told her grandparents what the bullies were saying to her.

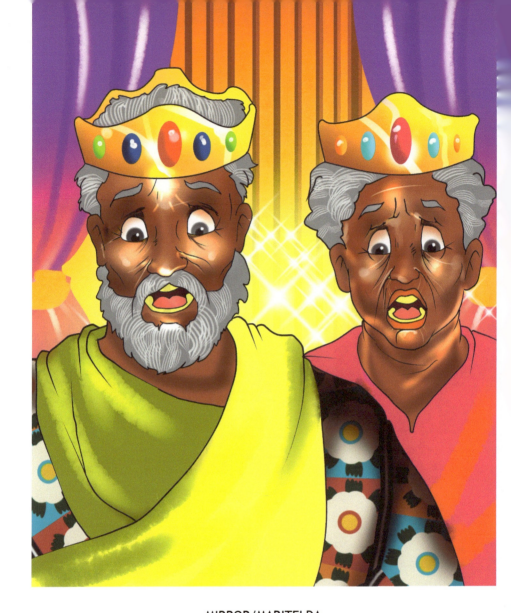

MIRROR/MARITELDA

One day, Evilida, the Wicked Witch, disguised herself as an old lady and appeared in Little Black Alice's magic mirror and spoke to her. "Go to the City of Manego, and request to see the King. He will grant you friends and give you the color of your choice. Just write a note to your grandma." Alice, excitedly looks in the mirror and asks, "what shall I say when I write to my grandma"?

Evilida, as the old lady responds, "start with Dear Grandma and Papa..."

Grandma, Grandpa, and Brown Sugar sit down for dinner. Grandma waits for Little Alice to come to dinner. The motor car broke down and although Little Alice understands the car broke down, she is still hurt that no one came to her competition. Grandpa scolds Brown Sugar for making an onion and garlic sandwich and not brushing her teeth. He tells her that she should never go outdoors without brushing her teeth and combing her hair. Brown Sugar says she's sorry. When Grandma goes to get Little Alice from her bedroom, she sees a letter on the kitchen counter. It is a letter from Little Alice. Grandma hurries to open it.

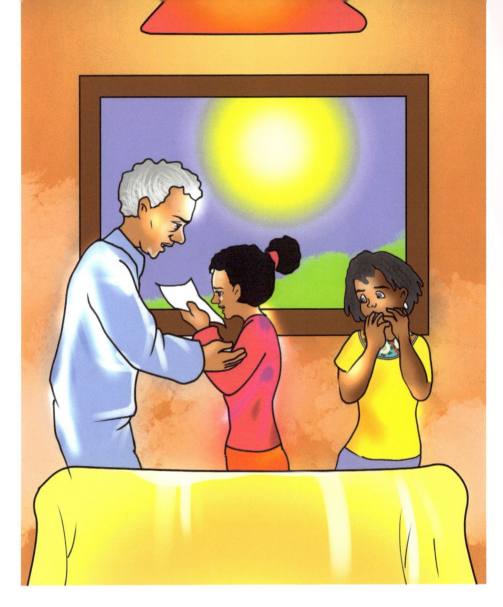

In the letter, Little Alice lets her Grandma and Grandpa know that she's going to see the King in Manego to get her color changed and learn how to make friends. Grandma cries and cries, feeling that Little Alice may never come back. Grandma Harris knows that Evilida kidnaps little black children for their souls. Brown Sugar finishes eating her onion cakes then runs upstairs to Little Alice's room to see what happened.

Now, inside the bedroom of Little Black Alice, Brown Sugar presses a button on the side of Little Alice's tall dressing mirror, which allows her to see what happened in Little Alice's bedroom in the last twenty-four hours. Brown Sugar is surprised to see what's happened.

When Brown Sugar looks in the mirror, she sees both Evilida and Dogoodie Goodie standing outside of the mirror. Brown Sugar hears what Maritelda, who is really Evilida dressed as an old lady tells Little Black Alice. She runs back to the kitchen to tell her Grandmother, who is still terribly upset. Brown Sugar tells her grandmother that Little Black Alice was tricked by the Wicked Evilida. I hope you are not as confused as I am telling you all this. Read it again if you are confused.

Grandma Harris and Grandpa Harris listen to Brown Sugar tell them what Evilida told Little Alice. Brown Sugar also says she saw Dogoodie the Good witch in the room with Little Alice. This was good news to Grandma and Grandpa Harris. That means, although something bad could happen to Little Alice because of Evilida's tricks, something good could happen because Dogoodie Goodie was there.

Remember, the light always takes over the dark; the good we do will always outlast the evil others do.

Evilida tricks Little Alice and tells her the King will send a magic carpet to pick her up at her school. While waiting for the King, Little Black Alice falls asleep on the school bench. Alice awakens to see the old lady from her mirror coming towards her. The old lady offers Little Alice candy as she waits on the magic carpet. Little Alice was told to never accept food from a stranger, but she is so tempted by the smell of the candy.

The Wicked Witch of Manego has put a spell on the candy Little Alice has eaten. Evilida's sister, DoGoodie Goodie, and Little Alice's sister, Brown Sugar, try to help Little Alice, but it's too late. Because Little Alice disobeyed her grandparents by eating something from a stranger, she is now under the wicked witch's zombie trance.

Even though Little Alice knew it was wrong to take the candy, she took it anyway. She thought that she could trust this little old lady. She tried not to remember that her Grandmother always told her not to give in to the temptation of eating snacks. As Little Alice felt the effects of the Digbiddy Root Candy affect her body, Little Alice remembered what her grandmother told her, when you are disobedient bad things can happen to us. Boy was her grandmother right.

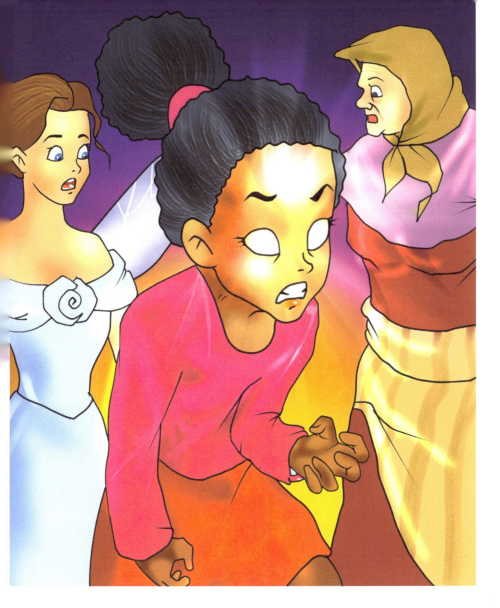

Accepting the candy and running away shows us how Little Alice made two wrong choices. We all must think about the choices we make at all times. Little Alice starts shaking and trembling. She's going into a trance. Brown Sugar and Dogoodie tell Little Alice to run. But Little Alice can't move her feet. Brown Sugar looks at her sister and realizes that she's not herself. Little Alice's eyes are open wide, and she doesn't blink.

Evilida laughs loud and tells Little Black Alice to say that she wants to go to Manego, and that she wants to be another color. Alice repeats and repeats these words over and over. Little Alice spins and spins in a circle as the Wicked Evilida twirls her hands, making Little Alice spin. She stops in front of Evilida with a blank mannequin- like stare. Little Alice is under Evilida's spell. Evilida continues to laugh uncontrollably. Tears flow from Brown Sugar's eyes.

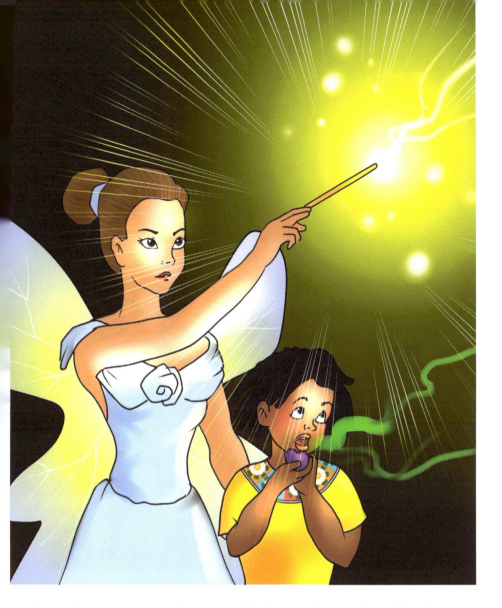

Dogoodie runs over to Alice and twirls her magic wand, readying it to yield a great magical spell. Brown Sugar crosses her fingers hoping that Dogoodie's magic wand will save Little Alice.

DOGOODIE

Oh, magic wand - my good luck charm
- save Little Alice from any and all harm
- take away Evilida's hold
and guard Alice from the soul patrol
- magic wand, please set free
- Little dancing Alice for me.

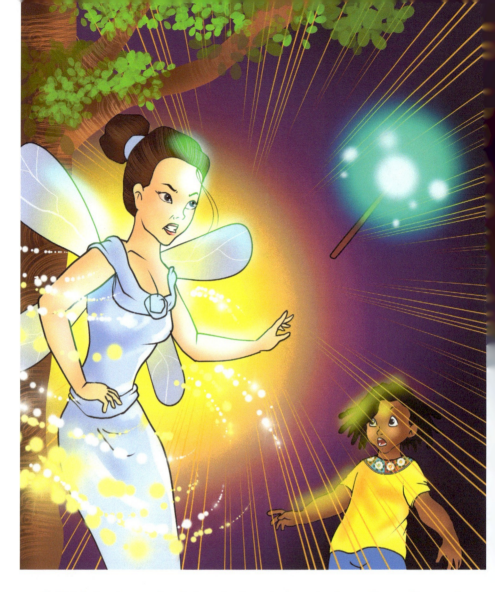

Evilida's loud gross laugh is out of control as she hears Dogoodie speak
her sweet but simple incantation.

EVILIDA

Don't you know that your magic is useless against the BLACK MAGIC
STONE OF MANEGO! (raising her arms) Let Mama evil show you
what real magic is. First I'll break that goody goody wand of yours.
(Evilida points the huge Black Magic Stone ring at Dogoodie's Wand.
Instantly, Dogoodie's wand fly's out of her hand and breaks in half.
Brown Sugar starts to cry again.)

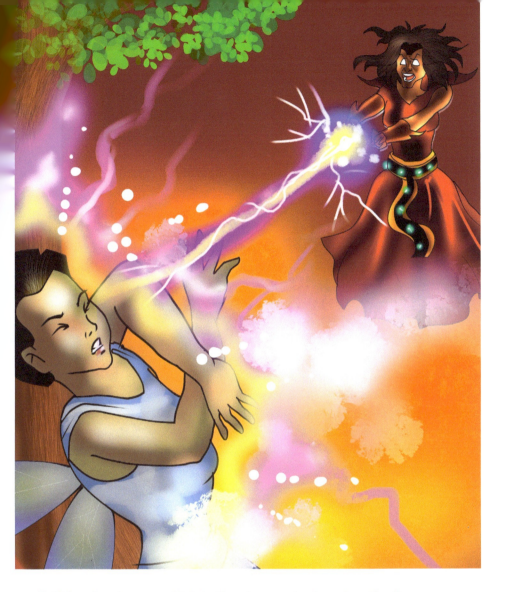

Evilida raises her arms high in the air exposing her claw like fingers as a gust of wind howls in the distance. Evilida starts her incantation....

> "Dark stone of Manego, blessed evil friend to me
> Here these evil words I speak to thee.
> I bid use of your spooky power
> To put the freeze on these two for an hour..."

HA HA HA HA HA. Evilida laughs and laughs as she realizes that Brown Sugar and Dogoodie are now temporarily frozen.

Evilida's Soul Patrol Captain flies down from a gray cloud and swoops Little Alice away to Manego, the Land of Colors. Evilida takes off with them without a magic carpet. She raises her ring up to the cloud and shoots off toward the sun, disappearing within the clouds. Brown Sugar and Dogoodie stand frozen looking at Little Black Alice taken away by the Soul Patrol Captain. Tears flow from Brown Sugar's beautiful eyes. Slowly, Brown Sugar is able to move her lips.

BROWN SUGAR

We have to save my sister. If she loses her skin color, she'll lose her soul and won't be able to dance again.

DOGOODIE

We will save her. But know, your soul has nothing to do with your skin color. We all have a soul. Our soul is our spiritual identity. Spirit has no color. My magic carpet is only equipped to fly one person. I'll meet you in Manego after my wand is repaired.

BROWN SUGAR

What if something should happen, like the Monster of Manego decides that I'm fit for his supper, or if one of the wicked witch's daughters tries to practice voodoo on me, or what if I get lost? What will I have for protection?

DOGOODIE

Your bad breath. (They instantly become unfrozen.)

Chapter 2 – I Want to Go Back Home

Evilida's Soul Patrol Captain drops Little Alice on the wrong side of Manego. Eating Ethel tries to wake Little Black Alice from her deep sleep but she doesn't wake up until she feels Walking Dog licking her cute, round face. Alice looks around, a bit frightened. She realizes she is no longer in Popadubop. Alice is surprised to see Walking Dog stand on two legs instead of four.

Alice introduces herself to Ethel. Ethel tells her she knows who she is, but they must get out of the area before Evilida, and her Soul Patrol find her. She tells her the Soul Patrol Captain dropped her on the wrong side of town. They are in Dogoodie Goodie territory, however, they are remarkably close to where Evilida's haunted palace is located. The Wicked Witch Evilida has three dirty little daughters, dirty because they don't bathe, she tells Alice, and a weird son named Creeplie, who likes to eat bugs and toe jam. Alice quickly says that Evilida's daughters sound like they are really bad news.

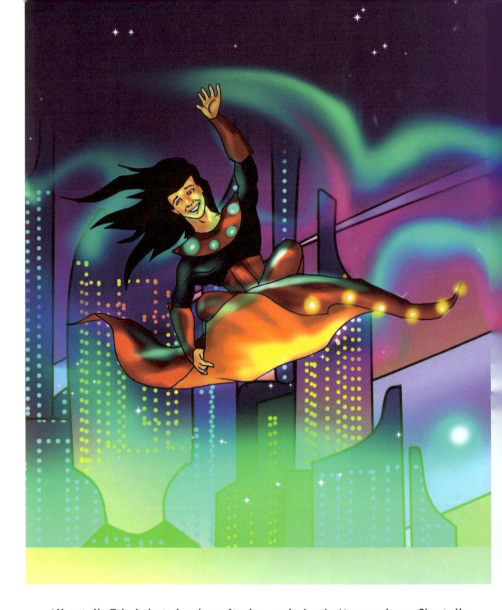

Alice tells Ethel that she doesn't plan on being in Manego long. She tells Ethel how kids call her names all the time, like nappy head, Kunta Crispy, and the shoe black girl. She explains how lonely she feels. She says that no one seems to understand her or know how she feels. Ethel tells her she used to be teased after Evilida hexed to make her never stop eating. She said children called her names like Eating Ethel, the fatty fat girl, or when she visited people, they would hide all the food in the house. Alice asks Ethel if her feelings aren't hurt. Ethel says not anymore. She says she doesn't care what people say, because she likes herself more than the words others say about her.

EATING ETHEL jumps rope with her automatic jump rope; Little Alice really likes the rope. Little Alice lets Ethel know that they don't have anything like that in Popadubop. Little Alice wants to find out how to be another color and to have friends. Ethel tells Little Alice the wicked Evilida makes promises she can't keep. She lets her know that once you get to Manego, you can't leave or see the king unless you beat her Soul Patrol. Evilida's Soul Patrol dancers have never been beaten. Alice realizes that she may never get home and may never see the king. Ethel tells Little Alice that she'll gladly switch colors with her, but it can be rather painful. Alice says it can't be more painful than being bullied.

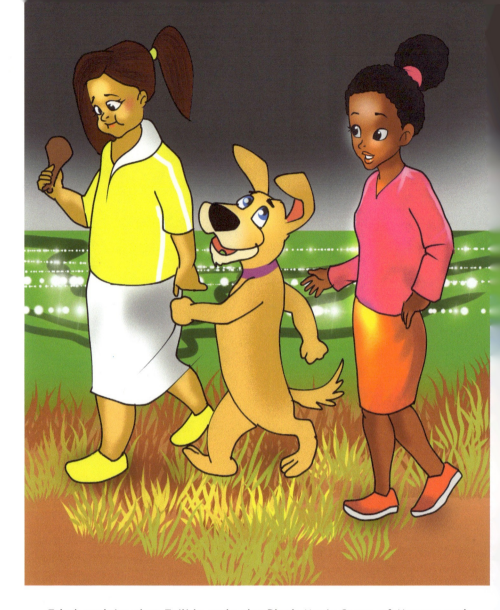

Ethel explains that Evilida stole the Black Magic Stone of Manego and changed all that was good to evil. Her plan was to create her own dance company after she learned all of Prince Manego's dance moves. Only the Prince didn't even like Evilida romantically. So, she tricked the best dancers to come here where she made them zombies. Little Alice realizes that she may become a zombie. She makes a deal with Ethel to switch colors with her and she wants Ethel to show her how to get to the King's palace to learn how to make friends so she can get back home. Ethel explains all the hoodoos Evilida has done, like making her never stop eating just because she was shaped better than her daughters.

Ethel tells Little Alice that Walking Dog was too friendly with everyone but her, so she hoodooed the dog to never walk on all fours which hurts his legs. And she explains that her brother, Langley, told the truth too much so Evilida hoodooed her brother to tell lies. So, Alice must remember to take everything Langley says and reverse it. Langley tells Alice that the Soul Patrol is rehearsing new dance steps to beat her when the competition comes. He reminds Little Alice that if she loses, she will never get home and she will become a zombie. This was a lot of information for Little Alice to reverse. As they continued walking, they heard a loud roar. It was the Monster coming out of the Digbiddy Lake.

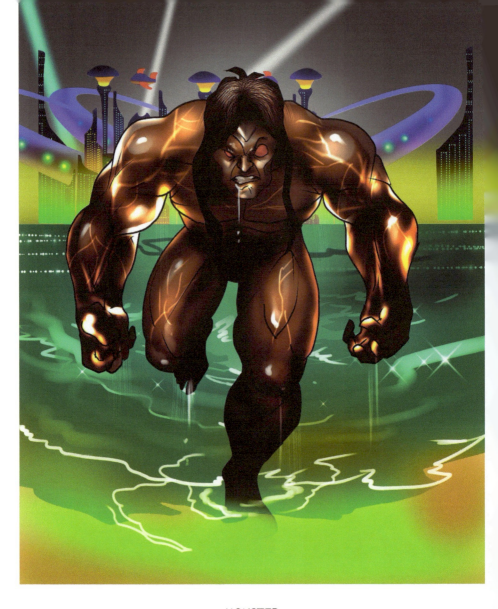

MONSTER

Growl.... Roar.... Growl...EEEaAAA.

Ethel grabs Alice by the hand and leads her away from the Monster's roar. She tells Alice that the Monster of Manego is loose and to come to her house. Alice insists on going to Digbiddy Lake to get her bag of clothes she left when she was dropped by the Soul Patrol Captain. Ethel's mother comes out to get Langley, the dog, and Ethel. She tells Alice to come with her. Ethel, Langley, and Walking Dog run amazingly fast to their home as the Monster's roar gets louder and louder, which means the Monster is getting closer and closer.

Ethel points in the direction of the lake with one hand and with the other hand she points to where she lives. The Monster roars loud again. As Little Alice runs toward the lake, the Monster grabs her.

ALICE

Noooooooooooooooo! GRANDMA.... SOMEDBODY HELP ME! I WANT TO GO HOME... HELP ME!

Chapter 3 – A Winner Who Cheats
Never Keeps the Prize

Hi there boys and girls. It's me, Simon the Storyteller. Oh, boy, Oh boy, Oh boy... I know you all know I know this story and I do. It's just that I forgot a little bit of it

(Relieved)

Oh, yea ... I have the storyteller card right here... We are now in the chambers of the meanest, the evilest, the ugliest witch in the galaxy... the one, the only - Evilida and her dancing daughters, Nagatha, Ragatha, and Hagatha.

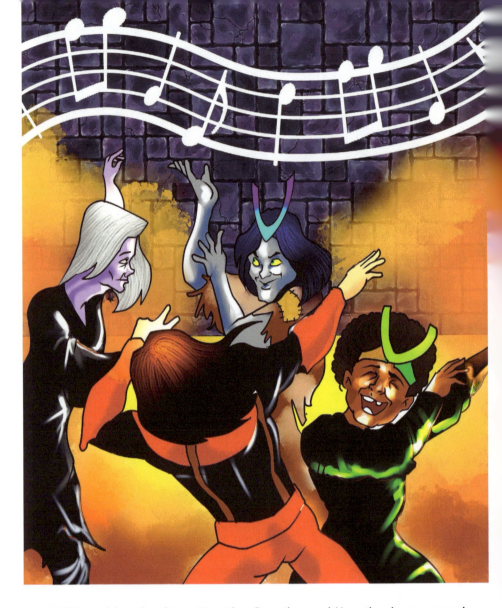

Evilida and her daughters Nagatha, Ragatha, and Hagatha dance around the cauldron in a ritual dance. Simon likes the beat of the wild music and dances with Evilida's brainless wild daughters. Simon dances with them, but he really shouldn't be in the scene with them. He's supposed to be telling you the story, but he loves to dance like Evilida's daughters.

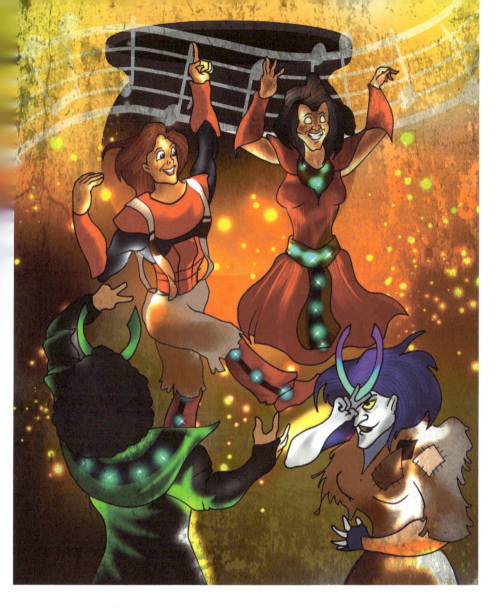

Evilida joins Simon and her daughters in the wild crazy dance all over the smelly dungeon. Simon doesn't realize that Evilida plans to kidnap him and hold him hostage until he tells her where Little Black Alice is hiding.

When he realizes that Evilida has tricked him, it's too late. Evilida's son, Creeplie, holds Simon over a cauldron which holds the dragon's toe and nail soup. Evilida commands Simon to tell her where Little Black Alice is hiding. Simon screams for help. He calls for Dogoodie to help him. He refuses to tell Evilida that Little Alice is being helped by the Monster.

(Dogoodie floats in Evilida's smelly chamber with little gift bags, waving her rose petaled wand. Creeplie releases Simon from his grip.)

CREEPLIE

I will get you one day, Mr. Storyteller (as he drools all over himself).

SIMON

Scram you creepy creep before I put another hump in your back.

(Simon flees out the window, escaping being put in the bubbling cauldron.)

Simon hurries out the window where his magic carpet awaits. He barely makes a getaway from Evilida's cauldron. Creeplie stomps out the smelly dungeon mad because his Aunt Dogoodie freed Simon. Simon realizes that it's important to follow directions. He was told to follow the story the way it was written. He was almost boiled in the cauldron for being disobedient. He learned he must respect wisdom.

Dogoodie Goodie daintily flies over to her three nieces and hands three beautiful gold wrapped boxes to each stinky little niece. The little witches jump up and down with excitement to receive the boxes from their Aunt Dogoodie. The little witches tear paper tops off the boxes at the same time. They smile as they take out the small, sweet-smelling bottles of perfume. Evilida runs to stop them but it's too late, they have already sniffed the scented perfumes.

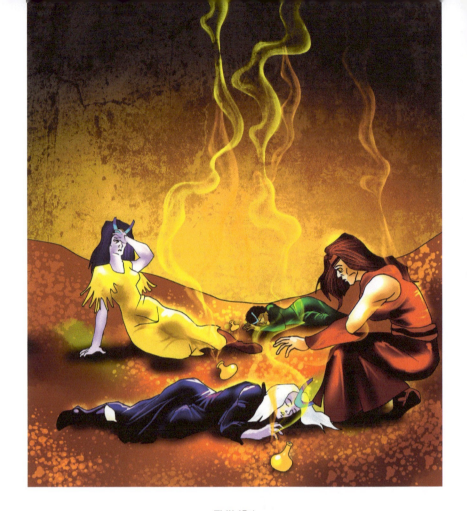

EVILIDA

PERFUME! PERFUME! Hold your noses, girls, like I taught you. Oh, drat it's too late. Dogoodie, why would you give my little girls perfume?

DOGOODIE

Little girls should brush their teeth. Little girls should wear clean clothes. And most importantly, little girls should always smell good.

(The little witches faint one by one.)

EVILIDA

Not my little girls. Get up! Get up, little witches, we have to find Little Black Alice, so I can hoodoo her to lose.

DOGOODIE

You will never find her in time. Remember, dear sister, a winner who cheats never keeps their prize.

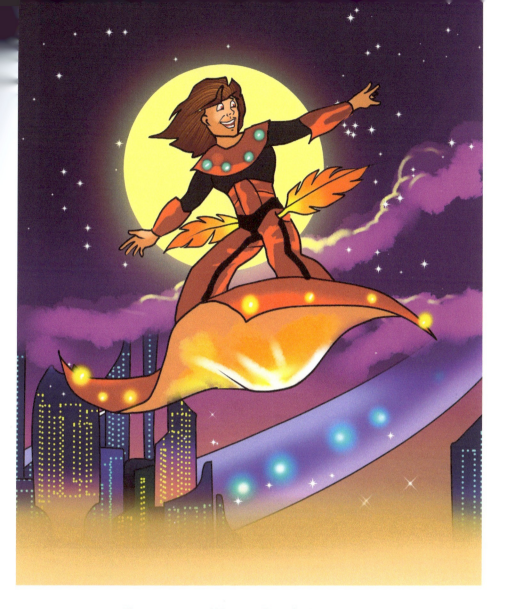

Chapter 4 – "Stop, Don't Leave Me Don't Let Him Take Me"

Boy, oh boy, gee whizzy whiz wow. Brown Sugar has arrived to save her sister but does not know where Dogoodie Goodie lives or where to look to find her. Langley and Walking Dog should be able to help her. Just so you know, the Monster didn't hurt Little Alice. Brown Sugar stands in the middle of the Road of Roads signpost and scratches her head as she hears Walking Dog tell her to reverse everything Langley says. The more Langley speaks, the closer she will be to figuring out where Little Alice is hiding.

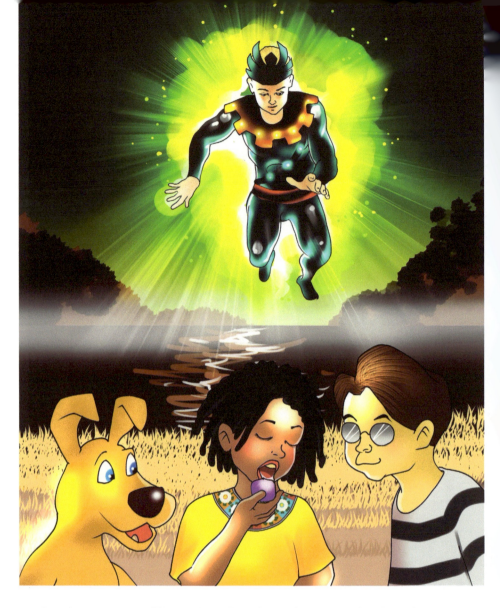

Langley eats part of Brown Sugar's garlic and onion sandwich as they wait on his sister Eating Ethel. Brown Sugar finds out that Little Black Alice was there on the lakes and then the Monster grabbed her. They start to walk toward the lake where the Monster took Alice when suddenly, over- head, the Soul Patrol Captain flies close to them. Langley and Walking Dog start running in fear of being picked up by the Soul Patrol Captain.

The Soul Patrol Captain mistakes Brown Sugar for Little Black Alice. Langley and Walking Dog run so fast that they leave a whirlwind of dust as they exit the Roads of Roads. Then, with one close fly into Brown Sugar, the Soul Patrol Captain swoops down and snatches Brown Sugar up by her arms. Brown Sugar screams at the Soul Patrol Captain to let her go. She begs Langley, "STOP, DON'T LEAVE ME... DON'T LET HIM TAKE ME..."

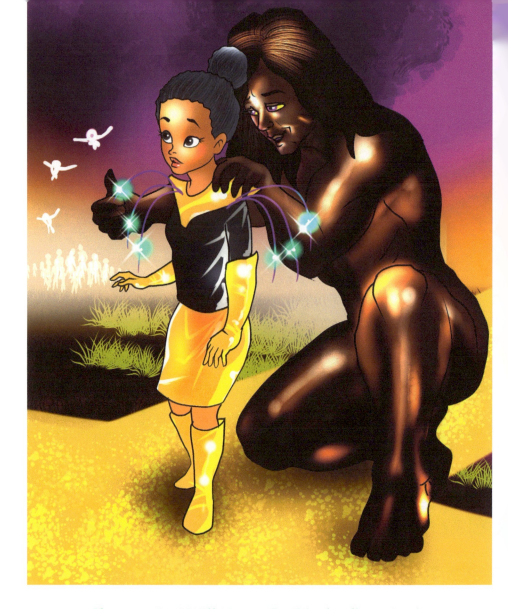

Chapter 5 – I Will Never Be Disobedient Again

The Monster scolds Alice for running away from home and tells her that Dogoodie Goodie has a plan to help her beat the Soul Patrol Army. The Monster explains that she must have faith in herself to beat the Soul Patrol Army, or she will be there in Manego forever. Alice admits that she made a poor choice by not listening to her grandmother and grand-father's advice. She promises the Monster she will never be disobedient again. She asks him how to have faith in yourself when you feel alone. He says that there is a power inside her that is with her always and she can never be alone. He tells her she must find that power within.

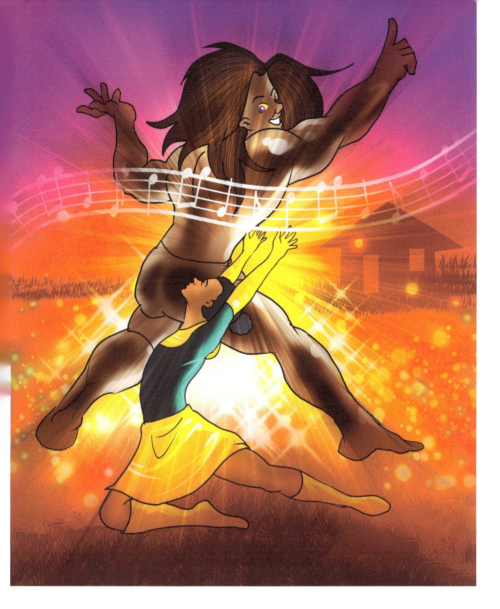

The Monster works with Alice on a very difficult dance combination that, if done correctly, could give her an advantage in beating the Soul Patrol Army Dancers. Alice doubts her dance abilities at first when she can't learn the dance combinations, but the Monster keeps telling her that she is a winner and to work hard on the dance combinations. After many hours of practice, Little Alice impresses the Monster with how well she does the dance steps.

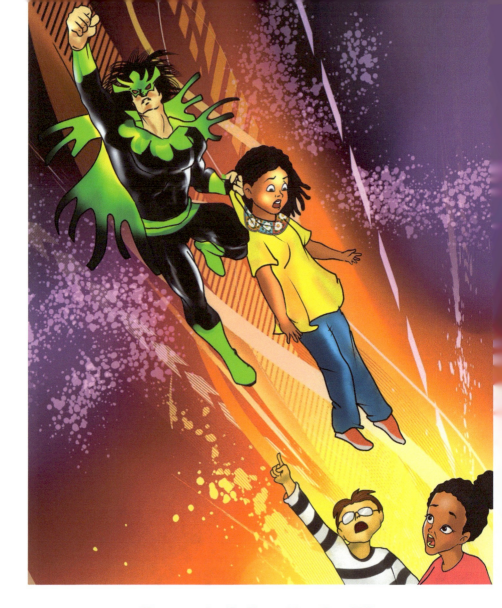

Chapter 6 – Believe You Can Win

As Alice goes to meet Dogoodie at Ethel's house, she runs into Langley and Walking Dog. In reverse, he tells Little Alice that the Soul Patrol Captain picked up Brown Sugar and carried her off. Little Alice looks up to see Brown Sugar trying to break free from the Soul Patrol Captain's grip. She is so happy to see her sister. Little Alice tells everyone that she has seen her sister and is worried that Evilida may kidnap her as well. Dogoodie lets her know that Brown Sugar is free and near her home. She tells Little Alice that Brown Sugar is important in her plan to trick Evilida.

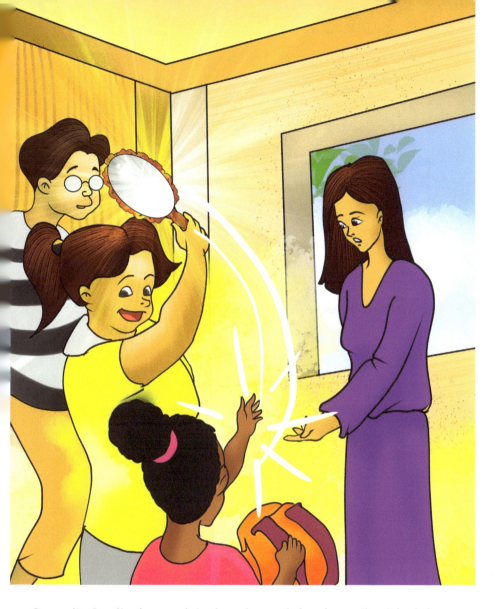

Dogoodie Goodie then explains her plan to defeat her evil, wicked sister Evilida to everyone present. Ethel, Langley, and Little Alice pay close attention to the details. Because Evilida outlawed anyone having mirrors, the fact that Little Alice brought one with her has everyone excited. Dogoodie will need the mirror to trick Evilida. Before the mirror is given to Dogoodie, everyone looks at themselves for the first time in years. They have fun laughing at how their faces have grown since Evilida took all the mirrors.

The Road of Roads

The Soul Patrol Dancers and Alice face each other on the Road of Roads. Langley, Dogoodie Goodie, Ethel and her mother, and Walking Dog look on as Little Alice warms up before she begins to dance. Ethel and her mother discuss that the Monster is really a good creature. They think about how many times they ran from him, not knowing he was really trying to tell them who he was. As the clouds move swiftly across the sky, they realize that Evilida is about to arrive.

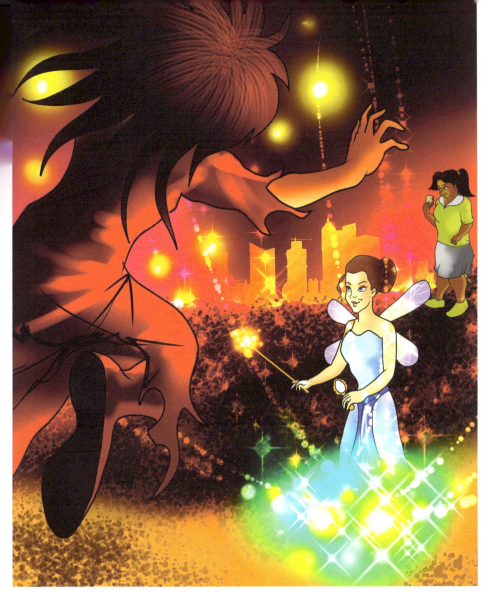

The sky darkens. The Earth starts to shake. Bolts of lightning soar through the sky. The townspeople stand still in fear as the Evil Evilida flies through the clouds on a bolt of lightning with electrical sparks coming from her hands and feet. As Evilida flies through the clouds, she screams an incantation that rumbles the Earth.

"Rain and stars, bewitching winds - bring up my dancers from the pit of Linds. Let them do dances that will tangle, the legs of this child I brought here to Manego. Ena' Rena' Micky - Moo, Ana' Cana' Kicki Poo. Oh, great evil - bring to my control, my invincible Soul Patrol."

The loud crackle of Evilida's loud laughter fills the heavens and shakes the Earth as she summons her Soul Patrol dancers. Her dancers fill the Road of Roads as they stand in a formation as they come out of cracks in the Earth, ride in on bolts of lightning from the sky, and from underneath the Manego bridge. At first, Little Alice has trouble keeping up with hard and fast movements from the dancers. The Soul Patrol dancers surround Little Alice, forcing her to lose her footing, then losing the beat of the music. The crowd looks sad as she struggles to keep up with the dance combinations. Evilida is excited to see Alice stumble. It looks like she's beaten, when suddenly she hears the roar of the Monster, who charges in.

MONSTER

You can beat them, Alice. Do the dance combinations I taught you.

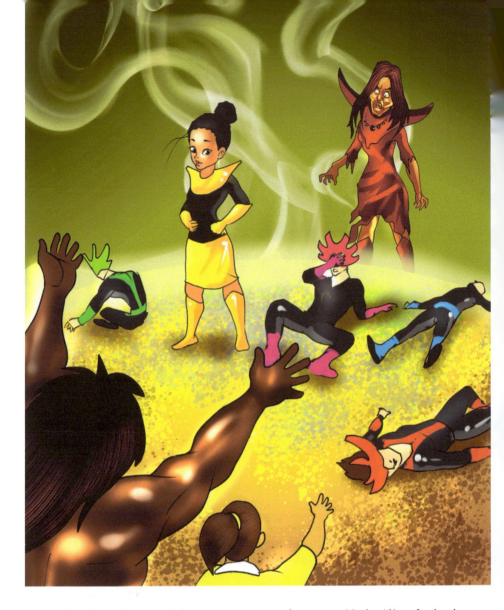

Little Alice dances with great power and energy. Little Alice feels the vibration of the music. Instantly, she remembers the combination that the Monster taught her and Alice comes alive in her dance. Little Alice dances on pointed toes, gracefully turning, twirling, and leaping without effort. As the Soul Patrol dancers try to repeat her dance steps, they fall at her feet. Alice leaps in the air with a perfect grand jeté.

The CROWD cheers Alice's victory. The town people realize with Alice's victory there is a possibility that Evilida may lose her power. Evilida is shocked at the loss of her Soul Patrol. Evilida goes to zap Little Alice. With her hands in a zapping position, Dogoodie Goodie distracts her with a loud, angelic laugh.

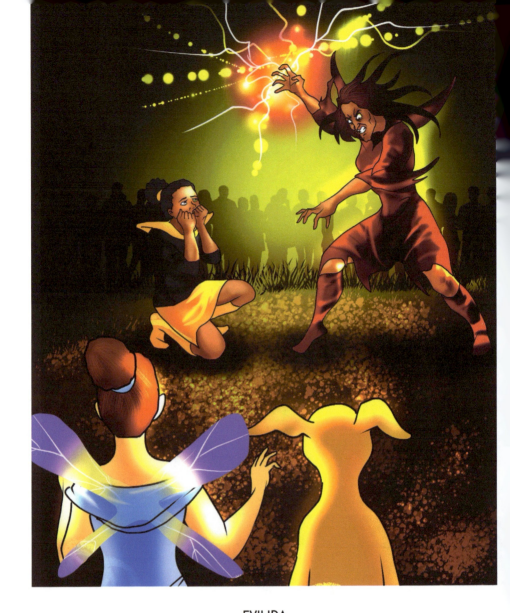

EVILIDA

I'm not in the mood, Dogoodie Goodie. DON'T CROSS ME. (Evilida holds up her zapping finger.)

(continuing)

Why... I'll zap you into the land of Mickey-Moo.

(electrical sparks spring from her finger)

Take that!

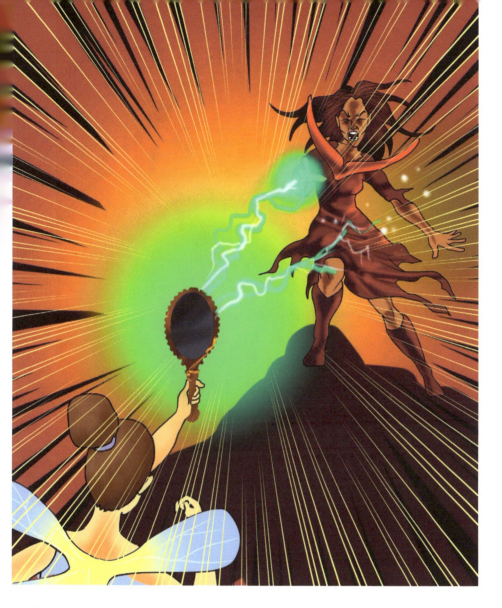

Dogoodie quickly holds up the mirror from Little Black Alice as Evilida raises her arms to zap her. Quickly, we see the zap bounce Evilida's electrical zap back to her and the Soul Patrol Captain.

Shocked that Dogoodie Goodie had the mirror, the Soul Patrol Captain and the wicked Evilida stand frozen. All the townspeople cheer with happiness and hope. Dogoodie places the mirror in Evilida's hand as Little Alice runs off with Ethel and Langley.

Chapter 7 – We Are All Born Perfect the Way We Are

SIMON

See, positive things can happen when you think positive thoughts. So, I thank all you wonderful readers for helping Little Alice make it here to the King's palace. Little Alice still has a few more problems she needs you to help her out with. She still hasn't seen the King and Queen. Also, she doesn't know where her sister Brown Sugar is being kept. So, please keep thinking good thoughts for Little Black Alice.

We are now in the palace of the King and Queen of Manego.

The King and Queen congratulate Alice on beating the Soul Patrol, but they tell her that they are so disappointed in her being disobedient to her grandparents. They tell her that coming to Manego was not a good decision. Alice tells them she wanted to learn to have friends and change colors and the Queen tells her that she will never have friends if she doesn't accept herself. Little Alice tells them the Monster said the same thing. They tell her the Monster is really their son. They tell Alice that for her and Brown Sugar to get home, they must get the Black Magic Stone of Manego and make Evilida cry.

Dogoodie Goodie speaks through the magic fountain and alerts the King; it's time to get Little Alice to the Road of Roads. They must confront Evilida before the sun goes down. Little Alice is told Dogoodie has found Brown Sugar, so she takes a shortcut to the Road of Roads. When Little Alice gets to the Road of Roads, her sister is being held by Evilida and her daughters. Brown Sugar breaks away when she sees her sister.

Alice tells Brown Sugar that she will never dance in Evilida's Soul Patrol. She tells Brown Sugar that she has taken her soul from one of her trophies and she now wants Brown Sugar to take it and swallow it to make sure Evilida will never have it for her Soul Patrol. Evilida stares at Little Black Alice as she whispers something important in Brown Sugar's ear. Brown Sugar nods her head several times then looks as if she's swallowed something. Evilida runs to Brown Sugar. She wants whatever Brown Sugar has swallowed.

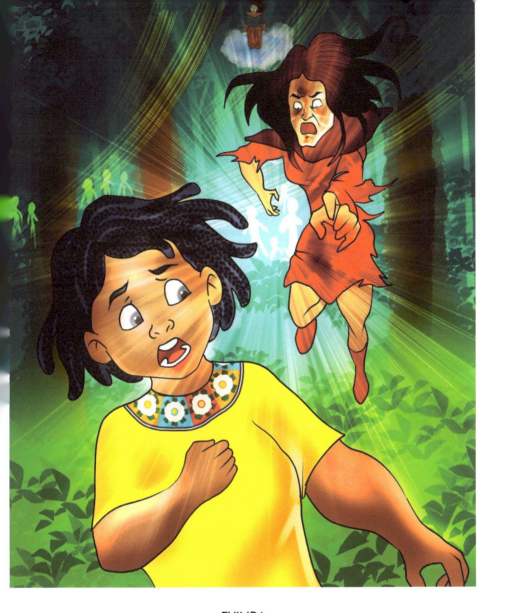

EVILIDA

What is that you've given her? What was that?

ALICE

My soul.

EVILIDA

Your soul? I must have it. Give it to me. I'll copy it. I must have her soul... give it to me.

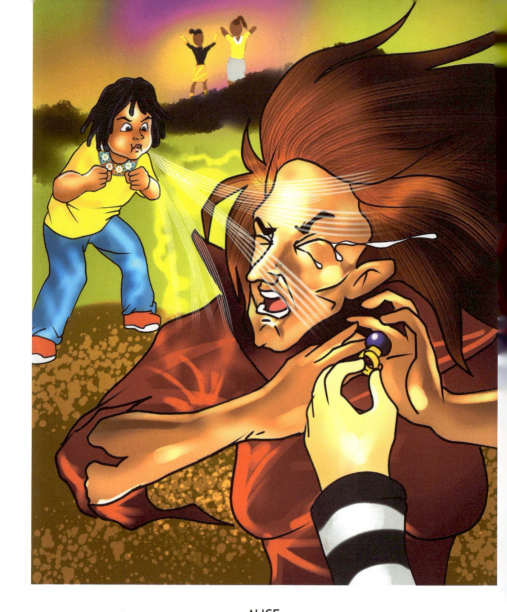

ALICE

Give it to her... open your mouth and give her all that good old
onion breath ... blow out all that bad breath.

EVILIDA

Onions, please not onions! Don't blow your onion breath on me.
You will destroy my evilness. OOH your breath is really funky
child, I'm about to pass out...

(Evilida falls crumpled on the ground and her three daughters faint one
by one.)

Evilida is now a regular person with no special powers. Walking Dog will now be able to walk on all four of his legs, and Langley will tell the truth and all the evil magic done by the wicked Evilida has disappeared. The spell is off of the town and all the townspeople. Ethel will now be able to eat like a normal person. And the Monster will be able to live without the horrible face Evilida cursed him with. Langley removes the Black Magic Stone from Evilida's finger and gives it to the Prince.

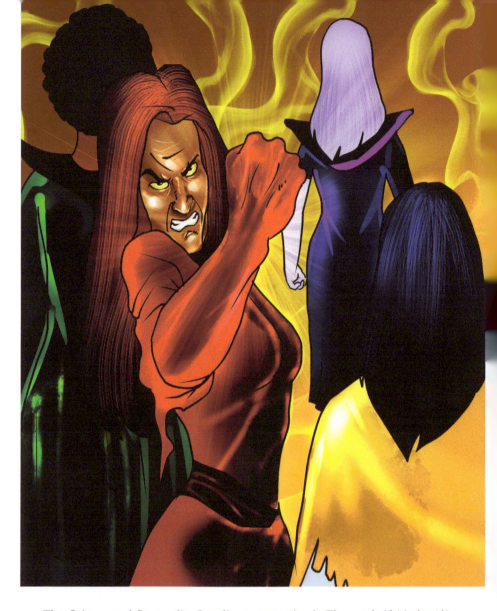

The Prince and Dogoodie Goodie are reunited. They ask if Little Alice and Brown Sugar are ready to go back to Popadubop. The Prince wants to know if Little Alice still wants to change her skin color as Dogoodie leads the witches to a large pool for bathing. Evilida tells Little Alice she will one day rule again so be aware this battle with her isn't over. Brown Sugar and Little Alice laugh as Evilida storms away with her daughters.

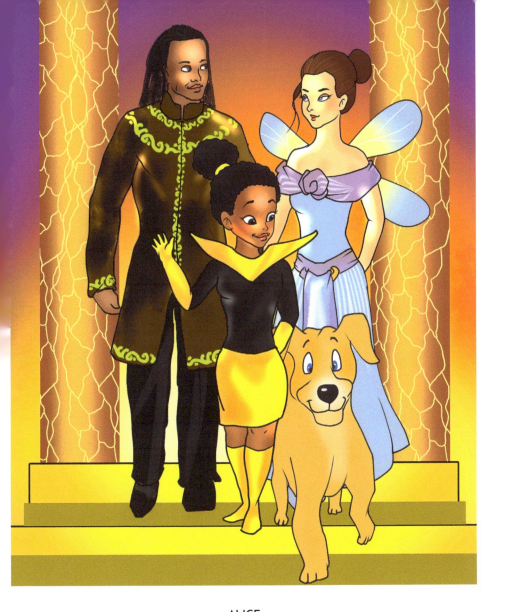

ALICE

I want to go back home the same color. I don't mean to break my promise with you, Ethel, but I wouldn't trade being black for anything. I made a big mistake making that wish. I'm glad I had the chance to meet new friends like you, Monster. I mean Prince Manego, and you Langley – you too Walking Dog.

(Ethel cries and runs to Dogoodie Goodie as she floats back in.)

ETHEL

You want to go home. You can't leave me...
You know you're my only real friend. Don't go Alice. Please don't
leave me. I thought we were friends.

ALICE

I'll always be your friend, Ethel, always... I'll write (exploding
into tears). Even if I'm old and gray. I could never stay away from
you, Ethel.

The Prince and Dogoodie let Little Alice and Brown Sugar know that it is time for them to get back to Earth before it gets too late. Dogoodie gives Little Alice the Black Magic Stone of Manego. Dogoodie believed or thought that the Black Magic Stone would not work on Earth. Little Alice thanks Dogoodie for all her help and tells her she will not be disobedient again. Little Alice doesn't want her color changed or anything else from Manego. She realizes her bad decisions. She wants to go home.
She misses her granny gran and her grandpa.

After they say goodbye, Dogoodie Goodie waves her magic wand and Brown Sugar and Alice start to fly through the clouds. She waves her wand a second time which will magically let Little Black Alice and Brown Sugar forget all that happened. Little Alice smiles and smiles as they fly the million miles back to Popadubop. Ethel cries and cries as she sees Brown Sugar and Little Alice fly away to another universe.

EXT. POPADUBOP HIGH

Brown Sugar wakes Little Alice up from her sleep on the school bench. She fell asleep on the park bench while waiting for Brown Sugar to pick her up. Little Alice just came from a school trip. Alice opens her hand and sees the Black Stone of Manego in it. She shows it to Brown Sugar. Brown Sugar tells her she must have been dreaming. Brown Sugar tells her there is no such place called Manego. There is no such person as Evilida. She takes the ring from Little Alice's hand and tosses it on the ground and tells her they are going to be late for dinner.

Alice says goodbye to her teacher. She asks about the school trip. She can't believe she has been dreaming. Her teacher tells her she has just returned from the skating rink. She and Brown Sugar start to walk home. She turns around and Evilida materializes as the Old Woman and picks up the ring.

Alice stops Brown Sugar from walking and tells her to look at Evilida picking up the ring. When Brown Sugar turns around Evilida has flown away. Brown Sugar keeps walking. Little Alice looks terrified.

Evilida (from the clouds)

Goodbye for now Black Alice. I shall see you soon, for I shall reign as the first EVIL QUEEN OF UNIVERSE! Ha Ha Ha Ha

The End of Book 1

Coming Soon - The Revenge of Evilida

CPSIA information can be obtained
at www.ICGtesting.com
Printed in the USA
BVHW020913170122
626429BV00001B/1